Best Start

MUSIC LESSONS

AURAL GAMES

A resource book of games and activities to develop aural skills in young musicians.

Sarah Broughton Stalbow

Best Start Publishing
www.beststartmusic.com

Available from **www.beststartmusic.com** and on Amazon.

First published in 2019 by Best Start Publishing

© Sarah Broughton Stalbow, 2019

ISBN: 978-0-6485764-5-7

The moral rights of the author have been asserted.

All rights reserved. Except as permitted under the Australian Copyright Act 1968 (for example, a fair dealing for the purposes of study, research, criticism or review), no part of this book may be reproduced, stored in a retrieval system, communicated or transmitted in any form or by any means without prior written permission.

All inquiries should be made to the author.

Cover art and text design by Sarah Broughton Stalbow, editing by Rob Stalbow.

A catalogue record for this book is available from the National Library of Australia

Best Start Publishing
www.beststartmusic.com

For Teachers and Parents

Ongoing development of aural skills is a fundamental aspect of music education. These are the skills a student needs to be able to keep a steady pulse and play in time with a strong sense of rhythm.

Well developed aural skills allow students to be able to:

- assess their own sound,
- self correct, and
- play in tune.

This book is intended to be used in conjunction with beginner instrumental music lessons, to develop aural skills and awareness as a regular part of each lesson. The activities are designed to be completed with a teacher during lessons and are suitable for both individual and group contexts. They are short and require very little pre-planning or organization, making them ideal for instrumental teachers to select quickly and as needed, during lessons.

The activities can be implemented without the need for props or additional percussion instruments, although if available, these can be used in some activities to add interest and variety. Teachers may wish to select aural activities to be used in conjunction with the introduction of specific concepts in instrumental lessons. The colour illustrations included in the book are for the benefit of the students. The teacher may use the visual images to help students comprehend the musical characteristics of the aural activities.

Teachers may choose to allocate five minutes of each lesson to an aural activity from this book. Teacher and student can take tuns to choose which activity to do, alternating each week. Giving students the opportunity to make a choice allows them to have some power and control over what they are doing, and this encourages autonomy.

Many activities mirror the aural test requirements in AMEB*, ABRSM** and Trinity College London music exams, thus providing preparation resources for students approaching their first music examinations. Regular exposure and practise of aural skills promotes students' musical development in so many ways, yet often these skills are neglected until just before a music exam!

There are many excellent references and resources available on the development of children's aural skills, particularly from the Kodaly associations. Also, there are many classroom music teachers who have developed excellent resources for aural development, particularly in using singing and movement to teach musical concepts. The activities in this book are also suitable for classroom music lessons or can be adapted with minimal effort, for the classroom context.

Further information and resources are available from the following organisations:
- International Kodaly Society: https://www.iks.hu/
- Kodaly Music Education Institute of Australia: http://www.kodaly.org.au/resources
- Dalcroze Australia: https://www.dalcroze.org.au/

* Australian Music Examinations Board

** Associated Board of the Royal Schools of Music

Contents

Developing Inner Hearing   **Page 8**
1. Heartbeat Call and Response
2. Silent Beats
3. Silent Heartbeat
4. Pass the Beat
5. Mary #1
6. Mary #2
7. Mary #3
8. Stop and Go

Music and Movement   **Page 11**
1. In the hall of the Mountain King
2. Dance of the Sugar Plum Fairy
3. Hedwig's Theme
4. O Fortuna
5. Danse Macabre
6. Rodeo
7. Waltz No.2
8. Syncopation
9. The Can Can

Pulse and Rhythm   **Page 16**
1. Call and Response Rhythms
2. Tempo (Speed) Change
3. Keep the Beat
4. Expressive Pulse
5. Follow the Leader
6. Partner Clapping
7. Miss Mary Mack
8. Sevens
9. Name Game
10. Feet and Hands #1
11. Feet and Hands #2
12. Feet and Hands #3

Solfege Singing   **Page 22**
1. First Intervals
2. Advanced Intervals
3. Fixed Doh - Copycats
4. Copycats - Leaving Out Notes
5. Hot Cross Buns - Moveable Doh
6. Twinkle Twinkle - Moveable Doh
7. Doh Mi Soh
8. Compose

Listening Skills   **Page 30**
1. High / Low
2. Jumping / Stepping
3. Major/minor - Happy/sad
4. Triple or Duple?
5. Listen - Clap - Sing
6. Step up or Down?
7. Step or Skip?
8. Echo Game
9. Song Detective
10. Scale Singing
11. Scale Detective
12. Chord Singing #1
13. Chord Singing #2
14. Part Singing
15. Expression Detective

Inner Hearing

Inner hearing (also known as "audiation") is being able to hear sounds, melodies, and words inside the head, without any external sounds present.

Developing inner hearing allows students to think in terms of pitch, rhythm, and eventually, harmony.

It is relevant to music literacy: it develops the "ear to eye" or "sound to symbol" process. Students understand what the sound is before they learn to read or write it, and music becomes a familiar vocabulary.

Development of inner hearing also builds a strong sense of pulse, and develops concentration and focus.

*1. Heartbeat Call and Response

Clapping activity in 4/4 time.

Divide into two groups and decide on a steady pulse.

1. Group 1 claps two beats: "1, 2"
2. Group 2 echoes, clapping two beats: "3, 4"
3. Repeat and maintain a steady pulse!

Try other variations such as:

- Group 1 claps three beats and Group 2 claps the fourth beat.
- Pass the beat - each person claps one beat.
- Do this activity using other key signatures eg 3/4 and 6/8.

*2. Silent Beats

1. Clap four crotchet beats: "1, 2, 3, 4"

   Continue clapping this rhythm.

2. Choose a beat to *think* silently - clap in your head, but not aloud.
3. Continue clapping, always being silent on the chosen beat.

To make it harder, each person can choose to be silent on a different beat.

Inner Hearing

*3. Silent Heartbeat

1. Count a steady beat out loud eg 1, 2, 3, 4
2. Whisper the beat.
3. Hear the beat internally (no sound).
4. Continue counting silently in your head and choose a beat to play on.
5. Make it harder: everyone choose a different beat to play on.

4. Pass the Beat

1. Each person claps once, passing the beat back and forwards (if there are two people) or around a circle (if there are a group of people).
2. Count each clap aloud up to eight, repeating and keeping in time.
3. Next, be silent on beat one - the person who gets beat one should stay silent for that beat, the beat continues to the next person who claps beat two, and so on continuing around the circle.
4. Next, be silent on beats one *and* two, and so on adding silent beats until finally you are only clapping on beat eight!
5. For small groups you could try doing this activity with a metronome to keep in time, and also to explore using different speeds.

*Adapted from Paul Harris, *Improve Your Teaching! Teaching Beginners: A new approach for instrumental and singing teachers* (Faber Music, 2008) 17

Inner Hearing

The following three "Mary" activities are adaptations of the folk song *There was a farmer had a dog...*

The song ends by spelling the dog's name: B-I-N-G-O and Bingo was his name-O. The song is repeated multiple times, the first repetition leaves out the B, the second repetition leaves out the B and the I, and so on. The singers have to imagine the letters in their head so that they come in with the last line together.

5. Mary #1

1. Sing the song *Mary had a little lamb* out loud.
2. Sing it again but leave out the word "lamb" every time you get to it.
3. Make it harder by adding another word to leave out each time you sing it!

You can do this activity with any familiar song such as *Happy Birthday, Hot Cross Buns...*

6. Mary #2

1. Sing the song *Mary had a little lamb* out loud.
2. Now sing it silently, mouthing the words, but with no sound coming out.
3. Hear the song *Mary had a little lamb* inside your head and clap whenever you get to the word *"lamb"*.
4. Make it harder by adding other words to clap on.

You can do this activity with any familiar song.

Inner Hearing

7. ## Mary #3

   1. Sing the song *Mary had a little lamb* out loud.
   2. Now sing it silently, mouthing the words, no sound.
   3. Hear the song inside your head - choose one word to sing out loud. Whenever you get to that word, sing it out loud, but keep all the other words silent!

8. ## Stop and Go

   1. Choose a familiar song such as *Happy Birthday* or *Hot Cross Buns*.
   2. Start singing it aloud.
   3. When the teacher holds up their hand like a stop signal, stop singing aloud, *but continue singing inside your head.*
   4. When the teacher puts their hand down, continue the song, singing out loud.
   5. Take turns at being the teacher.

Music and Movement

Movement to music helps children develop fine and gross motor skills, coordination, and listening skills. It fosters imagination and creativity, teaches children about expressing emotions, and can teach social skills (in group situations).

Listening and moving to music also develops a deep understanding and appreciation for music, it's expressive capabilities, form and structure, by using the whole body to feel the beat, and the whole body to express the character of the music. The pioneer of using movement to enhance music learning was Emile Jaques-Dalcroze.

The following are a few simple ideas which can be incorporated into a music lesson without too much pre-lesson planning, and without the need for props. There are many more resources available today which give detailed lesson plans for teaching musical concepts through movement exercises.

In addition to the ideas below, teachers could also use these listening exercises to talk about what instruments are playing, do they sound high or low, or discuss the timbre and character of the instruments. The only limits are your imagination!

1. In the Hall of the Mountain King

In the Hall of the Mountain King

by Edvard Grieg

Imagine a story - a troll lives alone in a cave in the mountain. It's night, it's dark, he's creeping through the forest surrounding his cave. He knows someone is there - but where are they? Who is it?! Get ready for a surprise at the end!!

When the music is quiet, make your body small and clap or tap quietly in time with the music.

As the music gets louders louder, gradually make your movements bigger and louder!

You might start sitting down or crouched low to the ground, and end up standing and running on the spot!

Music and Movement

2. Dance of the Sugar Plum Fairy

Dance of the Sugar Plum Fairy

by Pyotr Ilyich Tchaikovsky

Imagine a story: you are a mischievous fairy or an elf sneaking into the house at night to sprinkle magic and fairy dust.

Keep the beat with small fairy claps or tip-toes as you creep around careful not to wake anyone up. Look over your shoulder, has someone heard you?

When the music swirls, swirl your arms to sprinkle fairy dust everywhere.

As the music swirls higher and higher imagine your magic is making all of the furniture rise up into the air as you lift your hands up!

3. Hedwig's Theme

Hedwig's Theme: Prologue from Harry Potter and the Philosopher's Stone

by John Williams

Imagine you are an owl and a wizard has given you a magical letter to deliver. Flap your wings in time with the music as you fly throughthe air.

As the music swirls up high, swoop your arms up above your head.

Watch out for wolves or goblins trying to steal the letter!

When the music changes, imagine you have landed on a branch - scurry along a branch or windowsill in time with the music.

Music and Movement

4. O Fortuna

> *O Fortuna, Fortuna Iperatrix Mundi*
>
> *from Carmina Burana by Carl Orff*
>
> Listen for the singers: Ta Ta Ta Ta.
>
> Listen for the instruments in the background: Ti-ti, ti-ti, ti-ti, ti-ti.
>
> Listen for loud *(forte)* and soft *(piano)*.
>
> Imagine you are building a huge castle. Hammer the bricks down: Ta Ta Ta Ta.
>
> Use your fingers to scurry like mice: Ti-ti, ti-ti, ti-ti, ti-ti.
>
> Listen for the very loud crashes and clap your hands together - Crash! imagine your castle is under attack from an enemy…

5. Danse Macabre

> *Danse Macabre*
>
> *by Camille Saint-Saens*
>
> Listen for:
> - Solo violin
> - Orchestra (lots of instruments playing together)
> - Short, spiky music
> - Smooth, swaying music
>
> Make up different body movements for each character. For example, you could do jerky robot moves for the short, spiky *(staccato)* music, and swaying or rocking moves for the smooth *(legato)* music. Listen and change your movements in time with the music!

Music and Movement

6. Hoedown

Hoedown from Rodeo

by Aaron Copland

Aaron Copland was an American composer and this music is from his ballet "Rodeo", which tells the story of a cowgirl trying to fit in with the men. A hoedown (or barn dance) is part of a rodeo competition in the American West.

At a hoedown people do square dancing. Try some square dancing moves to this music! Notice how the music is in groups of 8 beats.

1. Standing in 2 lines facing each other, walk forward 8 steps then back 8 steps.
2. Join hands in a circle, walk to the right 8 steps then to the left 8 steps.
3. Link arms with your partner, skip around each other for 8 beats, then change directions and skip for 8 beats.
4. Do-si-do your partner for 8 beats one way and then the other.

7. Waltz

Waltz No. 2

by Dimitri Shostakovich

Have a go at waltzing - a three step pattern with your feet.

Also try different body percussion combinations in 3/4 time.

For example:

1	2	3	1	2	3	1	2	3	1	2	3
knees,	click right,	click left,	knees,	click right,	click left,	knees__(float hands up)			knees__(float hands up)		

Music and Movement

8. Syncopation

> Listen to these songs and clap the beat.
>
> Notice the SYNCOPATED rhythms.
>
> Often there is a strong emphasis or accent on notes that are not on the beat.
>
> 1. In the Mood by Glenn Miller
> 2. Take 5 by Dave Brubeck
> 3. The Rite of Spring - Sacrificial Dance by Igor Stravinsky

9. The Can Can

> *The Can Can*
>
> *by Jaques Offenbach*
>
> The Can Can is a high energy dance in 2/4 time that originated in France. It involves high kicks, swishing skirts, and often splits and cartwheels. It was originally danced by both men and women, however today it is usually danced by a chorus line of women.
>
> Learn how to do the Can Can!
>
> Beat 1 = Right knee lifts up and down.
>
> Beat 2 = Kick right leg up and across the body, and then down.
>
> Repeat on the left side!

Pulse and Rhythm

1. Call and Response Rhythms

Most children are familiar with the idea of call and response - the teacher claps a short rhythm and the student claps it back.

Rhythms can be relatively short initially, but can progress to longer and more complex rhythms as students become more advanced.

Rhythms using a range of different time signatures should be used.

You can use clapping, body percussion, or a mix of both.

Difficult rhythms in repertoire can be taught away from the music using call and response, repeating the rhythm until it is familiar.

2. Tempo (Speed) Change

This activity can use clapping or whole body movement.

1. Listen to music (either played by the teacher on an instrument or using pre-recorded music), and clap or walk in time with the tempo (speed) of the music.
2. The teacher will change the tempo of the music frequently!
3. Listen carefully - keep in time with the music when the tempo changes!

Pulse and Rhythm

3. Keep the Beat

1. Listen to a song, either played on an insturment or a recording.
2. Clap in time with it keeping a steady beat.
3. When the music stops, confidently keep on clapping the same steady beat.

4. Expressive Pulse

This simple activity harnesses creativity and imagination, and teaches about dynamics and expression in music. Doing this with a metronome ensures that a steady pulse is maintained even when the dynamics change.

1. Clap, tap, or stamp a steady pulse, in time with a metronime if one is available.
2. Use different parts of your body to feel the pulse.
3. Expression: try soft and loud, grumpy and dreamy - but stay in time with the pulse!
4. Make up a short story and tell it using sounds. For example, soldiers marching towards you from far away (*crescendo*), or rain falling and then a lightening flash, or a clock that ticks and chimes.

5. Follow the Leader

1. Decide on one person who will be the leader. This person should clap a steady beat.
2. The next person should join in clapping a simple ostinato (repeating rhythmic pattern).
3. When everyone has joined in clapping their own ostinato, follow the leader's DYNAMICS and EXPRESSION.

Pulse and Rhythm

Partner clapping is a traditional school ground activity, where children clap hands with each other in patterns, keeping a steady beat.

Partner clapping can be performed with just one partner, or with a whole group by standing in a circle and clapping hands with the people on either side.

As well as learning to keep a steady pulse, children learn concentration, coordination, and learn to work together.

6. Partner Clapping

Start facing your partner.
1. Clap your hands together 4 times.
2. Clap both of your hands together with your partner 4 times.
3. Repeat.

Make it harder.

Other combinations to try:
1. 2 claps + 2 partner claps.
2. 1 clap + 1 partner clap.
3. Slap knees, clap hands, clap hands with partner, clap hands again (4 beats in total).

Use different parts of the body and take turnes to create different combinations.

When clapping hands with your partner you can use the left and right hands separately, either clapping straight ahead (left hand to partner's right hand) or across the body (left hand to partner's left hand) to develop movement across the midline of the body.

Young beginners may like to say a rhyme as they clap to keep in time, for example *Miss Mary Mack* or *Pat-a-Cake*. There are some wonderful videos online which are easily found when searching for clapping games.

Pulse and Rhythm

7. Miss Mary Mack

A simple four beat clapping pattern:

1. Clap your hands together.
2. Clap your right hand to your partner's right hand (the movement will be across your body).
3. Clap your hands together.
4. Clap your left hand to your partner's left hand.

The words "Miss Mary" are an anacrusis or upbeat. Start your first clap on the word "Mack".

Tip: The repeated words (eg Mack, black, buttons etc) should always fall when you clap your hands together.

Miss Mary Mack, Mack, Mack,

All dressed in black, black, black,

With silver buttons, buttons, buttons,

All down her back, back, back.

She asked her mother, mother, mother,

For fifty cents, cents, cents,

To see the elephants, elephants, elephants,

Jump the fence, fence, fence.

They jumped so high, high, high,

They touched the sky, sky, sky,

And never came back, back, back,

Until the fourth of July, July, July.

8. Sevens

This clapping game is performed side by side and does not involve clapping hands with the other person.

Repeat each pattern twice. Count aloud to seven as you perform each pattern:

1. Hit the table (or floor) 7 times: hit, hit, hit, hit, hit, hit, hit.
2. Alternate hitting the table and clapping: hit, clap, hit, clap, hit, clap, hit.
3. Alternate hitting the table, clapping and snapping your fingers: hit, clap, snap, hit, clap, snap, hit.
4. Then: hit, cross hands and hit the table, normal hit (uncrossed hands), clap, snap, clap, hit.
5. Do it all forwards and then backwards, repeating each pattern twice.

Pulse and Rhythm

9. Name Game

1. Clap a steady beat.
2. Each person take a turn to say their name to the beat. Then say your favourite food, favourite colour, what you had for breakfast…
3. Make up silly sentences, but stay in time with the beat!
4. Can you figure out what rhythm names are used to say your name?

The following activities are inspired by the eurythmics of Emile Jaques-Dalcroze, and use the feet and hands performing different rhythms at the same time.

Dalcroze pioneered the idea of teaching music in a multi sensory way, and developed exercises for his students that he called *eurythmics*. He believed in teaching music and musical understanding through active rhythmic movement, so that students can feel and understand how music moves through space and time.

Dalcroze exercises can enhance musicianship, and improve coordination and concentration.

10. Feet and Hands #1

1. Keep the beat with your feet, walking on the spot: **Ta Ta Ta Ta** (crotchets).
2. Clap one **Ti-ti** (quavers).

   Keep your feet going!
3. When you can do one **Ti-ti**, try clapping two or more in a row.
4. Keep adding ti-tis until you are consistently clapping quavers with your hands while walking crotchets with your feet.

Pulse and Rhythm

11. Feet and Hands #2

1. Keep the beat with your feet: **Ta ta ta ta** (crotchets).
2. Clap **Great Big Whole Notes** (semibreves) with your hands.
3. Clap **Ta-a** (minims) with your hands.
3. Then clap **Ti-ti** (quavers) with your hands.

You can stop and reorganise yoursef in between each new rhythm, but keep your feet walking to a steady beat while you clap!

Make it harder:

1. Choose two or three rhythm values to switch back and forth between eg **Ta-a** (minims) and **Ti-ti** (quavers).
2. Keep the beat with your feet: **Ta ta ta ta**
3. Clap **Ta-a** (minims)
4. When the teacher says "change", clap **ti-ti** (quavers)
5. When the teacher says "change" again, switch back to clapping **Ta-a** (minims).

12. Feet and Hands #3

1. Walk on the spot to a steady beat.
2. The teacher will call out a rhythm value to clap (eg crotchets).
3. Keep clapping that rhythm until the teacher calls out the next rhythm value to change to (eg semiquavers).

   This time you will not know what rhythm your teacher will call out next, so you have to concentrate on listening as well as keeping the beat!
4. Your feet should keep a steady beat the whole time!

Solfege Singing

Singing songs using solfege note names comes from the Kodaly method of music education, and is often used to teach pitch and sight singing. A solfege syllable is given to each note of the musical scale: doh - re - mi - fah - soh - lah - ti - doh. The Kodaly approach develops aural training through the use of folk songs, singing games, and folk dances, using solfege syllables to teach students about pitch, intervals, and harmony.

There are two ways to use solfege:
Fixed doh - doh is always the note C, re is always D, and so on. This teaches absolute pitch.
Movable doh - doh is always the tonic of the song. For example, in the key of G major, G would be doh, and in C Major, C would be doh. This teaches about the relationships between pitches.

Solfege singing is a useful tool for any student learning a musical instrument. Solfege singing:
- increases pitch awareness, including intonation,
- . develops an understanding of tonality,
- . develops sight reading skills,
- . helps develop the ability to self correct.

Solfege Singing

The Kodaly method uses specific hand signals for each solfege note name. For the purpose of instrumental music lessons it can be useful to use any hand gestures (not necessarily Kodaly hand gestures), that show the movement of pitch going up and down. The use of hand gestures helps provide a multi sensory approach to learning, using the ears to hear pitch, hand gestures for the body to "feel" the music, and the eyes to "see" the pitch going up and down. Hand gestures can be particularly useful for students who:

- . find singing in tune difficult,
- . find aural work challenging,
- . have not yet learned to read music,
- . find it difficult to concentrate.

Using a piano is very helpful when teaching solfege singing, but is not absolutely necessary.
If using a piano, the teacher can play and sing the melody, and can also add a basic chordal accompaniment if they wish. If there is no piano available, the teacher can sing the notes unaccompanied, but be sure to sing in tune!

Solfege Singing

1. First Intervals

The teacher may demonstrate these first intervals by playing them on the piano and singing the solfege syllable. The student then sings the interval back. It is easy to start with fixed doh, using the C Major scale.

You may choose to perform basic hand gestures which show the direction of the pitches going up and down.

To extend the activity you may like to make up other words to sing using the first intervals.

First intervals, performed as a call and response between teacher and student/s:

1. First notes   soh mi soh
2. Tritonic   soh mi lah
3. Tetratonic   doh mi soh lah
4. Pentatonic   doh re mi soh lah
5. Major hexatonic   doh re mi fah soh lah
6. Major   doh re mi fah soh lah ti doh

Extension activity - make up your own words to the same patterns of notes:

1. Call: "Are you here?"   Response: "I am here"
2. Call: "What's your name?"   Response: "I am _____"
3. Call: "Sit down quietly"   Response: "Sitting quietly"
4. Call: "Who is here today?"   Response: "I am here today"
5. Call: "Can you climb a ladder?"   Response: "I can climb a ladder"
6. Call: "What's for breakfast I am hungry!"   Response: "Toast and cornflakes fruit and yoghurt!"

Solfege Singing

2. Advanced Intervals

Sing intervals of the Major scale.

Use hand gestures to show the notes stepping higher.

Sing the interval first, then fill in the notes in between:

1. Doh - re;
2. Doh - mi   -   doh re mi
3. Doh - fah -   doh re mi fah
4. Doh - soh -   doh re mi fah soh
5. Doh - lah -   doh re mi fah soh lah
6. Doh - ti   -   doh re mi fah soh lah ti
7. Doh - doh -   doh re mi fah soh lah ti doh

Transition to recognising intervals:

The teacher plays an **interval**, the student must sing it back, and **work** out what interval it is by singing up the scale.

Solfege Singing

3. Fixed Doh - Copycats

This is a call and response activity combining an awareness of pitch, rhythm, and developing listening skills, and memory. Using fixed doh (doh is middle C on the piano) and the notes of the C Major scale, the teacher sings a short pattern of notes using solfege note names. The student sings the pattern back to the teacher.

Some example patterns of notes are provided below, but teachers can make up any pattern of notes they wish.

Best Start Music Book 1: For Teachers provides examples of simple patterns with piano accompaniment.

Listen and then sing:
- Doh re mi
- Re mi fah
- Mi fah soh
- Soh, fah mi re
- Soh fah mi re doh

Try some more Doh Re Mi patterns!

Listen and then sing:
- Doh re mi fah soh
- Soh lah soh
- Soh, lah ti doh
- Doh ti lah
- Ti lah soh
- Soh fah mi re doh

Try some more Doh Re Mi patterns!

Listen and then sing:
- Doh re mi fah soh
- Soh lah soh
- Soh lah ti doh
- Lah soh soh fah mi
- Soh mi doh

Try some more Doh Re Mi patterns!

Solfege Singing

4. Copycats - leaving out notes.

> Repeat the previous Copycats activity, but this time the teacher does not sing the solfege note name for the last note of each phrase. Students must listen and work out which note name to sing.
>
> When students become familiar with this activity, the teacher may progressively omit more and more of the solfege note names, so that eventually a student can hear a tune played on the piano (or other instrument) and sing the note names.

The following two movable doh activities can be done using any well known tune. After singing the tune, students can have a go at playing it on their instument, using their ears to find the right notes. Depending on how advanced the student is, they may be able to play the tunes on their instrument in several different keys!

5. Hot Cross Buns - Movable Doh

> Sing this song in C Major:
>
>   Mi re doh,
>
>   Mi re doh,
>
>   Doh doh doh doh
>
>   Re re re re
>
>   Mi re doh.
>
> You can actually start singing this song on any pitch, give it a go!

Solfege Singing

6. Twinkle Twinkle - Movable Doh

Twinkle Twinkle in solfege:

> Doh doh soh soh lah lah soh,
>
> Fah fah mi mi re re doh,
>
> Soh soh fah fah mi mi re,
>
> Soh soh fah fah mi mi re,
>
> Doh doh soh soh lah lah soh,
>
> Fah fah mi mi re re doh.

Sing it starting on different pitches. You can even try playing it on your instrument!

7. Doh Mi Soh

Learn this song in solfege:

> Doh mi soh soh lah lah soh__
>
> Doh mi soh soh fah mi re__
>
> Doh mi soh soh lah lah soh__
>
> Fah fah mi mi re re doh__

Sing it STACCATO and then LEGATO.

Now sing it starting on a different pitch.

Solfege Singing

8. Compose

Make up your own song using solfege note names.

Here is a good plan for writing a simple song:

>Line 1 - a simple melody using between 4 to 8 notes
>
>Line 2 - exactly the same as line 1, except for one difference ie change a note or a rhythm.
>
>Line 3 - different from the first two lines
>
>Line 4 - exactly the same as line 1

Expression

How do you want this song to sound?

Staccato or *legato*?

Forte or *piano*?

Happy or *grumpy*?

Extension

Play your tune on your instrument.

Write the notes of your tune on the musical staff, making sure to notate your chosen expression (eg staccato or dynamics).

Listening Skills

1. High / Low

Listen to some notes or a tune played on any instrument.
1. If they are HIGH notes, stand and stretch your arms up high.
2. If they are LOW notes, crouch down low.

2. Jumping / Stepping

Listen to some notes or a tune played on any instrument.
1. If the notes STEP smoothly, walk very carefully and smoothly.
2. If the notes JUMP from low to high (or high to low), jump up and down!

3. Major / minor - Happy / sad

Listen to the chords played on the piano.

If it sounds happy (Major), stand up straight with arms above your head.

If it sounds sad (minor), crouch down or touch your toes.

Listening Skills

4. Triple or Duple?

Swaying music has 3 beats in each bar (triple).

Marching music has 2 in each bar (duple).

1. Listen to the music.
2. Is the beat in groups of 3 or 2?
   Is it swaying music or marching music?
3. Sway or march in time with the music!

5. Listen - Clap - Sing

1. Listen carefully to a short melody.
2. Clap the rhythm back as an echo.
3. Listen to the melody again.
4. Now sing it!

6. Step Up or Down?

1. Listen to two notes.
2. Now sing them.
3. Do they step up, or step down?
3. Play two notes on your instrument, stepping up.
4. Play two notes on your instrument, stepping down.

Listening Skills

7. Step or Skip?

A step is the interval of a second.

A skip is the interval of a third.

1. Listen to two notes.
2. Sing the notes.
3. Do they step or skip?
4. Up or down?

8. Echo Game

1. Turn around so that you can't see the teacher.
2. Listen to the teacher play a note - it can be any note you have learned.
3. Find the note on your instrument so that you are echoing your teacher!

9. Song Detective

Teacher plays a known piece eg *Hot Cross Buns*, but changes something - it could be a different note or a changed rhythm.

Students identify the change.

After doing this with known songs, the teacher can play a short unfamiliar melody twice. When playing it a third time, the teacher can make a change, asking the students to identify the change.

Listening Skills

10. Scale Singing

1. Listen to your teacher play a major scale.
2. Sing a major scale using movable doh (ie sing doh re mi fah soh lah ti doh starting on any note that is comfortable to sing).
3. Now listen to your teacher play a minor scale.
4. Sing a minor scale using movable doh.
5. What sounds different about these two scales? How would you describe the character of each scale (eg happy, sad, lonely etc)? (Hint: listen carefully to the 3rd and 7th notes of the minor scale)

11. Scale Detective

The teacher plays a scale.

The student states whether it is major or minor.

12. Chord Singing #1

The teacher plays a two note chord (dyad) on the piano - two notes played together at the same time, within the limit of an octave.

1. Sing the higher of the two notes and put your hands on your head.
2. Sing the lower of the two notes and touch your toes.

Listening Skills

13. Chord Singing #2

The teacher plays a three note chord (triad), within the limit of an octave, on the piano.

Sing the notes of the chord from top to bottom:

1. Sing the highest note and put your hands on your head.
2. Sing the middle note and put your hands on your hips.
3. Sing the lowest note and touch your toes.

14. Part Singing

The teacher will play two, two-note chords (dyads) on the piano, one immediately following the other.

Sing the top notes of each chord.

15. Expression Detective

Listen to a melody played once.

Identify the dynamic - is it *forte* or *piano*?

Identify the expression (or articulation) used - is it *staccato* or *legato*?

www.ingramcontent.com/pod-product-compliance
Lightning Source LLC
Chambersburg PA
CBHW042142290426
44110CB00002B/89